COFFEE

RECIPES

HOT AND COLD COFFEE AND ESPRESSO BEVERAGES TO MAKE AT HOME

SARAH SPENCER

ISBN: 9798653352829

Printed in the United States

www.thecookbookpublisher.com

CONTENTS

INTRODUCTION

Coffee is something that keeps us going through the day. For some people, it is just a drink that will wake you up, but for some others, it's a whole religion. Those people are not only there to get coffee for a caffeine buzz but to really enjoy its irreplaceable flavor.

If you are a true coffee lover, then this cookbook is something you will enjoy. It has everything from super delicious caramel and hazelnut coffees to robust espresso and smooth latte recipes that will tickle your taste buds.

In this cookbook, you will find 25 cold and 25 hot coffee recipes. All of them are carefully created to make sure that every coffee lover can indulge in them. You can drink them with your breakfast, with your snack during the day, for a coffee break, or just for pure pleasure.

No matter if you drink your coffee with milk or not, you will find a recipe perfect for you with different flavors— from caramel and vanilla flavors to chocolate and hazelnut yumminess. If you are a big fan of the most world-famous coffees, you will find a perfect recipe for how to make it in your home. We have the famous Dalgona coffee in three different flavors, some popular copycat coffee recipes from favorite coffee shops, and even homemade brewed coffee flavor combinations that will be perfect for you and your friends. Most of the recipes in this cookbook are made with just plain coffee or strong espresso, but you will find some instant coffee and cappuccino recipes too.

There are two main types of coffee—Arabica and Robusta. The better-quality coffee is Arabica because the beans are roasted more and there's more intense flavor. The best tip for buying a great coffee is to know the origin of the coffee beans. Brazil, Somalia, Ethiopia, and Kenya have the best quality coffee in the world. If you are buying coffee and the origin is unknown, then that's probably not good quality coffee. Also, the quality varies depending on the date the coffee beans were roasted. You don't want coffee roasted more than 2–3 weeks ago.

If you want to keep your coffee fresh, you should store the ground coffee and coffee beans in an airtight container in your kitchen pantry away from direct light, heat, and moisture. To keep the best quality in the coffee, use it as soon as the package is open.

We all know how important it is to have our first coffee in the morning to start our day. Having this cookbook will help you to come up with super delicious coffee combinations that you would never imagine as summer-friendly and super refreshing iced coffees during hot weather.

Coffee happens to be the most popular drink in the world. Over time, the way it is prepared has changed and different flavor combinations have been developed.

For many, coffee happens to be the most important drink and the one you are not able to start a day without because it's what keeps you going during the day. There are so many different types of coffee that even the most experienced coffee drinkers are struggling with their choices. If you are a new coffee addict and don't know that much about this drink, you probably don't know how many possible ways and variations there are to enjoy this drink.

If you weren't addicted to coffee already, you will surely become a new coffee lover after tasting even one of the coffee flavors shown in this cookbook. No matter if you choose to make a hot or chilled coffee drink, latte or Frappuccino, coconut or hazelnut flavor, you are going to fall in love with those flavor combinations.

Many of the recipes can even be served with an extra topping of your choice. For a lot of the iced or hot coffee flavor combinations, you can put some extra chocolate, caramel or fruit sauce on top, or use ice cream to make it creamier and richer. By experimenting in the kitchen, even making coffee, you can come up with your own signature recipes to be proud of. Don't hesitate to try it; maybe you will be surprised what flavor combination you will come up with.

Some of the recipes ask for foamed milk, which can be made in a milk frother. You can absolutely use whole milk in the coffee recipes, but you can also use almond milk or coconut milk—even hazelnut milk will work fine. However, I will highly recommend using whole, full-fat milk because it gives a nice rich flavor and it froths well.

Most of the recipes in this book ask for brewed espresso as the base, but you can use your favorite coffee instead. If you are vegan or vegetarian, you can replace all the whole milk used in the recipes with almond milk or coconut milk. Any plant-based milk will work just fine. If the recipe doesn't include any sweetener and you have a sweet tooth, then you can sweeten your coffee with sugar, agave, honey, or maple syrup.

These foolproof recipes will show you how easy it is to enjoy the most popular and best-known coffees. They can all be made easily in your kitchen. You will be surprised how powerful a drink you can create with water, milk, and some ground coffee beans. Don't think anymore—just grab your coffee machine and start brewing some coffee.

ICED COFFEE RECIPES

Iced Vanilla Latte

One of the most desired coffee flavor combinations. I love how this coffee is ready in no time and gives a nice refreshing beginning to every day.

Serves 1 | Prep. time 10 minutes

Ingredients
1 cup brewed espresso, cold
¼ cup whole milk
1 teaspoon vanilla extract
5 ice cubes

Directions
1. Add the espresso, milk, and vanilla to a pitcher.
2. Mix until combined and pour into a serving glass filled with ice.

Nutrition (per serving)
Calories 99, fat 2 g, carbs 15 g, sugar 14.9 g, Protein 2 g, sodium 37 mg

Iced Green Tea Latte

If you are a tea lover and you want your tea to be nice and chilled, then this one is what you are looking for. Ready in just no time, it can cool you down on a hot summer day.

Serves 1 | Prep. time 10 minutes

Ingredients
1 cup milk
2 teaspoons matcha powder
1 tablespoon agave syrup
½ teaspoon vanilla extract
5 ice cubes

Directions
1. Add the matcha powder and a little bit of the milk to a pitcher.
2. Mix until dissolved and then stir in the rest of the milk and vanilla.
3. Mix until combined and pour into a serving glass filled with ice.

Nutrition (per serving)
Calories 222, fat 5 g, carbs 29.1 g, sugar 11.3 g, Protein 18 g, sodium 139 mg

Cinnamon and Caramel Latte

Caramel in coffee is a match made in heaven, especially when all of that is empowered by the magic taste of cinnamon.

Serves 1 | Prep. time 10 minutes

Ingredients
½ cup brewed espresso, cold
½ cup whole milk
2 tablespoons dolce de leche
¼ teaspoon cinnamon
5 ice cubes
¼ cup heavy whipping cream
1 teaspoon powdered sugar

Directions
1. Add the whipping cream and powdered sugar to a bowl and whip with a hand mixer until stiff peaks form.
2. Combine the espresso, milk, dolce de leche, and cinnamon in a big glass.
3. Add the ice cubes and mix thoroughly.
4. Decorate the glass with whipped cream.
5. Sprinkle some cinnamon on top and serve.

Nutrition (per serving)
Calories 293, fat 15.1 g, carbs 36.3 g, sugar 8.9 g, Protein 5.3 g, sodium 225 mg

Mocha Frappuccino

Decadent, delicious, and super easy to make. Let your next morning coffee be different and much tastier.

Serves 1 | Prep. time 10 minutes

Ingredients
¾ cup strongly brewed espresso, cold
½ cup whole milk
3 tablespoons chocolate sauce
5 ice cubes
¼ cup heavy whipping cream
1 teaspoon powdered sugar

Directions
1. Add the whipping cream and powdered sugar to a bowl and whip them with a hand mixer until stiff peaks form.
2. Combine the espresso, milk, and chocolate sauce in a big glass.
3. Add the ice cubes and mix thoroughly.
4. Decorate the top of the glass with the whipped cream.
5. Drizzle some extra fudge on top.

Nutrition (per serving)
Calories 389, fat 20.1 g, carbs 44.7 g, sugar 28.8 g, Protein 7.3 g, sodium 287 mg

Salted Caramel Frappuccino

A yummy and decadent salted caramel Frappuccino like you have never tasted before. Super refreshing and easy to make.

Serves 1 | Prep. time 10 minutes

Ingredients
½ cup brewed espresso, cold
2 tablespoons caramel sauce
Pinch of salt
½ cup milk
Ice cubes for serving
¼ cup heavy whipping cream
1 teaspoon powdered sugar

Directions
1. Add the whipping cream and powdered sugar to a bowl and whip them with a hand mixer until stiff peaks form.
2. Combine the espresso, caramel sauce, salt, and milk in a big glass.
3. Add the ice cubes and mix thoroughly.
4. Decorate the top of the glass with the whipped cream.
5. Drizzle some extra caramel sauce on top.

Nutrition (per serving)
Calories 279, fat 13.7 g, carbs 36.4 g, sugar 8 g, Protein 5.4 g, sodium 371 mg

Classic Iced Frappe

Super classic but very decadent and popular during the hot days of summer.

Serves 1 | Prep. time 10 minutes

Ingredients
1 tablespoon instant coffee
3 tablespoons water
1 tablespoon sugar
½ cup milk
5 ice cubes

Directions
1. Use a large blender or wire whisk to blend the instant coffee, water, and sugar together until thick foam forms.
2. Mix the foam with the milk and serve in a glass filled with ice cubes.

Nutrition (per serving)
Calories 106, fat 2.5 g, carbs 18 g, sugar 17.5 g, Protein 4 g, sodium 59 mg

Iced Chocolate Frappe

Chocolate frappe, easy to make, and very refreshing. It will keep you strong during the day.

Serves 1 | Prep. time 10 minutes

Ingredients
1 tablespoon instant coffee
3 tablespoons water
1 tablespoon sugar
½ cup milk
2 tablespoons chocolate sauce
5 ice cubes

Directions
1. Use a large blender or wire whisk to mix the instant coffee, water, and sugar together until thick foam forms.
2. Mix the foam with the milk.
3. Drizzle some sauce on the sides of the serving glass.
4. Fill the glass with ice cubes, add the coffee, and serve.

Nutrition (per serving)
Calories 239, fat 5.9 g, carbs 41.9 g, sugar 30.7 g, Protein 5.8 g, sodium 191 mg

White Chocolate Mocha

If you are a white chocolate lover, then this smooth and nice chilled coffee is everything you need to keep you on your feet for the day.

Serves 1 | Prep. time 10 minutes

Ingredients
½ cup brewed strong espresso, hot
2 ounces white chocolate, chopped
½ cup milk
5 ice cubes
¼ cup heavy whipping cream
1 teaspoon sugar
Pinch of nutmeg

Directions
1. Add the white chocolate to the hot espresso and let it melt.
2. Stir in the cold milk and pour the mixture into a serving glass filled with ice cubes.
3. Use a hand mixer to whip the whipping cream and sugar.
4. Decorate the serving glass with whipped cream and sprinkle with nutmeg.

Nutrition (per serving)
Calories 489, fat 31.9 g, carbs 44.6 g, sugar 43.1 g, Protein 8.1 g, sodium 146 mg

Peanut Butter Frappuccino

For all the peanut butter lovers out there, this one is for you. I am sure you are going to love it and enjoy it.

Serves 1 | Prep. time 10 minutes

Ingredients
1 teaspoon espresso
½ cup water
2 tablespoons honey
½ cup milk
2 tablespoons smooth peanut butter
5 ice cubes
¼ cup heavy whipping cream
1 teaspoon sugar
1 teaspoon chocolate sauce

Directions
1. Brew the espresso in a coffee machine.
2. Add the honey and peanut butter to the glass with the hot brewed espresso.
3. Add the cold milk.
4. Fill a serving glass with ice cubes and add the coffee mixture.
5. Add the whipping cream and sugar to a bowl and whip them with a hand mixer.
6. Decorate the serving glass with whipped cream and optionally a drizzle of chocolate sauce on top.

Nutrition (per serving)

Calories 520, fat 30.3 g, carbs 55.7 g, sugar 49.2 g, Protein 13.2 g, sodium 124 mg

Dalgona Coffee

A new trend for making delicious iced coffee that will inspire you to make your coffee more creative.

Serves 1 | Prep. time 10 minutes

Ingredients
1 tablespoon instant coffee
1 tablespoon sugar
¼ cup water
1 cup whole milk
5 ice cubes

Directions
1. Use a wire whisk to whip the instant coffee, sugar, and water.
2. Pour the milk and ice cubes into a glass and top the glass with the whipped coffee mixture.
3. Serve immediately.

Nutrition (per serving)
Calories 192, fat 7.9 g, carbs 23 g, sugar 24.8 g, Protein 7.9 g, sodium 100 mg

Dalgona Coconut Coffee

The famous Dalgona coffee has a new dimension. Flavored with a perfect amount of coconut, this is going to be super delicious for all the coconut lovers out there.

Serves 1 | Prep. time 10 minutes

Ingredients
1 tablespoon instant coffee
1 tablespoon sugar
¼ cup water
1 cup whole milk
2 tablespoons shredded coconut
5 ice cubes

Directions
1. Use a wire whisk to whip the instant coffee, sugar, and water.
2. Pour the milk and coconut into a blender and blitz until combined and smooth.
3. Transfer the milk mixture into a glass, fill it with ice cubes, and top with the whipped coffee mixture.
4. Serve immediately.

Nutrition (per serving)
Calories 227, fat 11.3 g, carbs 24.6 g, sugar 25.5 g, Protein 8.2 g, sodium 102 mg

Dalgona Chocolate Coffee

The famous Dalgona coffee has a new dimension. Flavored with a perfect amount of cocoa, this is going to be super delicious for all the chocolate lovers out there.

Serves 1 | Prep. time 10 minutes

Ingredients
1 tablespoon instant coffee
1 tablespoon sugar
¼ cup water
1 cup whole milk
2 tablespoons cocoa powder
5 ice cubes

Directions
1. Use a wire whisk to whip the instant coffee, sugar, and water.
2. Pour the milk and cocoa powder into a blender and blitz until combined and smooth.
3. Transfer the milk mixture into a glass, fill it with ice cubes, and top with the whipped coffee mixture.
4. Serve immediately.

Nutrition (per serving)
Calories 251, fat 12.7 g, carbs 30.5 g, sugar 25.6 g, Protein 10.2 g, sodium 104 mg

Double Chocolate Chip Cookie Frappuccino

Super delicious with chocolate chip cookies!

Serves 1 | Prep. time 10 minutes

Ingredients
½ cup strong espresso, cold
¼ cup chocolate chips
½ cup milk
2 chocolate chip cookies
5 ice cubes
¼ cup heavy whipping cream
1 teaspoon sugar
1 tablespoon chocolate sauce

Directions
1. Mix the espresso, chocolate chips, milk, and cookies in a blender.
2. Add the coffee to a serving glass filled with ice cubes.
3. Whip the whipping cream and sugar with a stand mixer.
4. Decorate the serving glass with whipped cream and a drizzle of chocolate sauce.

Nutrition (per serving)
Calories 629, fat 36.8 g, carbs 66.4 g, sugar 37.8 g, Protein 10.7 g, sodium 303 mg

Birthday Frappuccino

With all of the sprinkles on top, you'll be all ready to celebrate your birthday with this fabulous coffee.

Serves 1 | Prep. time 10 minutes

Ingredients
½ cup espresso, cold
½ cup milk
1 cup ice cubes
2 tablespoons hazelnut syrup
1 teaspoon vanilla extract
2 scoops vanilla ice cream
1 tablespoon sprinkles

Directions
1. Mix the espresso, milk, ice cubes, hazelnut syrup, and vanilla in a blender.
2. Add the coffee to a serving glass and top it with the ice cream.
3. Decorate the glass with a few sprinkles.

Nutrition (per serving)
Calories 468, fat 25.2 g, carbs 49.1 g, sugar 43.4 g, Protein 10.1 g, sodium 188 mg

Keto Frappuccino

This one is for all of you Keto lovers out there. I am sure that you are going to enjoy this coffee.

Serves 1 | Prep. time 10 minutes

Ingredients
½ cup espresso, cold
½ cup cream
5 ice cubes
1 teaspoon vanilla extract
¼ cup heavy whipping cream
1 tablespoon stevia

Directions
1. Add the cold espresso and cream to a serving glass filled with ice.
2. Mix in the vanilla and whip the whipping cream and stevia with a hand mixer or wire whisk.
3. Decorate the glass and serve.

Nutrition (per serving)
Calories 195, fat 17.8 g, carbs 5.1 g, sugar 3 g, Protein 1.7 g, sodium 77 mg

Caramel Brulee Latte

This French-inspired coffee is super delicious. It's easy to make at home and super enjoyable with friends and family.

Serves 1 | Prep. time 10 minutes

Ingredients

½ cup espresso, cold
½ cup cream
5 ice cubes
2 tablespoons caramel sauce
¼ cup heavy whipping cream
1 tablespoon caramel sauce for serving

Directions

1. Add the cold espresso, cream, ice cubes, and caramel sauce to a blender and blitz until smooth.
2. Transfer to a serving glass.
3. Whip the whipping cream and caramel sauce with a hand mixer and decorate the glass with the whipped cream.
4. Decorate the glass with an additional drizzle of caramel sauce.

Nutrition (per serving)

Calories 555, fat 31.8 g, carbs 58.1 g, sugar 38.4 g, Protein 8 g, sodium 308 mg

Gingerbread Latte

The perfect latte for the holiday season.

Serves 1 | Prep. time 10 minutes

Ingredients
½ cup espresso, cold
1 cup milk
5 ice cubes
2 tablespoons simple syrup
½ teaspoon ground cinnamon
½ teaspoon ground ginger
¼ teaspoon ground nutmeg
¼ cup heavy whipping cream
Pinch of ground ginger

Directions
1. Add the cold espresso, cream, ice cubes, simple syrup, cinnamon, ginger, and nutmeg to a blender and blitz until smooth. Transfer to a serving glass.
2. Whip the whipping cream with a hand mixer or wire whisk and decorate the glass with the whipped cream.
3. Decorate the glass with an additional pinch of ground ginger.

Nutrition (per serving)
Calories 364, fat 16.4 g, carbs 48.2 g, sugar 11.2 g, Protein 8.9 g, sodium 182 mg

Affogato Iced Coffee

A little ice cream makes all the difference. This Italian affogato coffee will please all your senses.

Serves 1 | Prep. time 10 minutes

Ingredients
1 cup brewed espresso, cold
2 scoops vanilla ice cream

Directions
1. Add the cold espresso to a serving glass and top it with two scoops of vanilla ice cream.
2. Serve and enjoy.

Nutrition (per serving)
Calories 279, fat 14 g, carbs 32 g, sugar 28 g,
Protein 4.9 g, sodium 140 mg

Eggnog Latte

If you miss eggnog, then this coffee latte will satisfy all your cravings for it.

Serves 1 | Prep. time 10 minutes

Ingredients
½ cup espresso, cold
¼ cup cream
½ cup eggnog
1 teaspoon vanilla extract
5 ice cubes
¼ cup heavy whipping cream
1 teaspoon powdered sugar
Pinch of nutmeg

Directions
1. Add the cold espresso, cream, eggnog, and vanilla to a serving glass filled with ice.
2. Mix until combined.
3. Whip the whipping cream and powdered sugar with a hand mixer and decorate the glass with the whipped cream.
4. Decorate the glass with an additional pinch of ground nutmeg.

Nutrition (per serving)
Calories 339, fat 24 g, carbs 23.1 g, sugar 15 g, Protein 6.1 g, sodium 126 mg

Caramel Apple Spice Coffee

This caramel apple spice coffee will tickle your taste buds and you will ask for another cup.

Serves 1 | Prep. time 10 minutes

Ingredients
½ cup espresso, cold
1 cup apple juice
5 ice cubes
3 tablespoons caramel sauce
¼ cup heavy whipping cream
1 tablespoon powdered sugar
Pinch of cinnamon
1 tablespoon caramel sauce for serving

Directions
1. Add the cold espresso, apple juice, and caramel sauce to a serving glass filled with ice.
2. Mix until combined.
3. Whip the whipping cream and powdered sugar with a hand mixer and decorate the glass with the whipped cream.
4. Decorate the glass with an additional pinch of ground cinnamon and drizzle of caramel sauce.

Nutrition (per serving)
Calories 566, fat 18.5 g, carbs 97.6 g, sugar 49.9 g, Protein 4.9 g, sodium 343 mg

Rum Flavored Ice Coffee

A little rum in your cup of coffee makes all the difference. Delicious, easy, and super quick to prepare.

Serves 1 | Prep. time 10 minutes

Ingredients
1 cup brewed espresso, cold
3 tablespoons cream
5 ice cubes
2 tablespoons brown sugar
1 tablespoon dark rum

Directions
1. Add the cold espresso, cream, brown sugar, and rum to a serving glass filled with ice.
2. Mix until the sugar is dissolved.
3. Serve and enjoy.

Nutrition (per serving)
Calories 128, fat 2 g, carbs 18.8 g, sugar 18.2 g, Protein 0.6 g, sodium 60 mg

Iced Mocha Coffee

With the right amount of coffee and cocoa powder, this coffee is super refreshing during hot summer days.

Serves 1 | Prep. time 10 minutes

Ingredients
1 cup brewed espresso, cold
5 ice cubes
1 teaspoon vanilla extract
2 tablespoons cocoa powder
½ cup milk

Directions
1. Add the cold espresso to a serving glass and top it with the ice cubes and vanilla.
2. Blitz the milk and cocoa powder in a high-speed blender.
3. Pour into the serving glass and mix until combined.
4. Serve and enjoy.

Nutrition (per serving)
Calories 102, fat 3.9 g, carbs 12.5 g, sugar 6.2 g, Protein 6.2 g, sodium 103 mg

Raspberry Iced Coffee

Fruity flavor with coffee is always a good idea. Especially when it comes to raspberries—they pair great with coffee.

Serves 1 | Prep. time 10 minutes

Ingredients
½ cup brewed espresso, cold
5 ice cubes
½ cup raspberries
2 tablespoons sugar
1 teaspoon vanilla extract

Directions
1. Add the cold espresso to a serving glass and top it with ice cubes and vanilla.
2. Blitz the raspberries and sugar in a high-speed blender. Strain through a fine-mesh sieve.
3. Pour the raspberry liquid into the glass with the coffee.
4. Serve and enjoy.

Nutrition (per serving)
Calories 136, fat 0.4 g, carbs 31.9 g, sugar 27.3 g, Protein 0.9g, sodium 27 mg

Cherry Iced Coffee

Cherries, like raspberries, are a great fruit to pair with coffee. This flavor combination is super delicious and easy to make.

Serves 1 | Prep. time 10 minutes

Ingredients
1 cup brewed espresso, cold
5 ice cubes
3 tablespoons cherry syrup
½ teaspoon vanilla extract

Directions
1. Add the cold espresso to a serving glass and top it with ice cubes and vanilla.
2. Stir in the cherry syrup and mix until combined.
3. Serve and enjoy.

Nutrition (per serving)
Calories 203, fat 0 g, carbs 48.3 g, sugar 48.3 g, Protein 0.3 g, sodium 43 mg

Caramel Frappe Coffee

This caramel coffee is super cool for summer days. It will refresh you and deliver the right amount of sweetness for a productive day.

Serves 1 | Prep. time 10 minutes

Ingredients
2 teaspoons instant coffee
¼ cup water
1 tablespoon sugar
5 ice cubes
½ cup whole milk
2 tablespoons caramel sauce

Directions
1. Blitz the instant coffee, sugar, and water in a blender.
2. Add the ice cubes to a serving glass and fill it with the coffee mixture.
3. Pour in the milk and drizzle with caramel sauce.
4. Serve and enjoy.

Nutrition (per serving)
Calories 222, fat 4 g, carbs 44.5 g, sugar 18.4 g, Protein 4.6 g, sodium 194 mg

HOT COFFEE RECIPES

Caramel Macchiato

This delicious warm coffee will please all your taste buds with its bursting flavor.

Serves 1 | Prep. time 10 minutes

Ingredients
2 teaspoons ground espresso coffee
1 cup hot water
¼ cup whole milk
1 teaspoon vanilla extract
1 tablespoon caramel sauce

Directions
1. Brew the espresso in a coffee machine.
2. Warm the milk in a small saucepan and froth it with a frother.
3. Add the brewed coffee to a serving glass and mix it with the caramel sauce and vanilla.
4. Add the milk foam on top.

Nutrition (per serving)
Calories 105, fat 2 g, carbs 16.8 g, sugar 3.7 g, Protein 2.6 g, sodium 130 mg

Cinnamon Dolce Latte

This delicious cinnamon flavored coffee is super easy to make and it's bursting with flavor.

Serves 1 | Prep. time 10 minutes

Ingredients
¾ cup boiling water
2 teaspoons instant espresso powder
½ cup milk
¼ teaspoon ground cinnamon
¼ teaspoon nutmeg
½ tablespoon powdered sugar
¼ cup heavy whipping cream
Pinch of cinnamon

Directions
1. Add the boiling water and espresso powder to a serving glass.
2. Mix and stir in the milk, ground cinnamon, and nutmeg.
3. Whip the whipping cream and powdered sugar and top the glass with whipped cream.
4. Decorate with a pinch of cinnamon.

Nutrition (per serving)
Calories 185, fat 13.8 g, carbs 11.6 g, sugar 9.6 g, Protein 4.7 g, sodium 75 mg

Mocha Coffee

This delicious mocha flavored coffee is super easy to make and it's bursting with flavor.

Serves 1 | Prep. time 10 minutes

Ingredients
2 teaspoons ground espresso coffee
1 cup water
1 tablespoon chocolate sauce
¼ cup milk

Directions
1. Brew the espresso coffee in a coffee machine.
2. Add the espresso to a serving glass and mix it with the chocolate sauce.
3. Stir in the milk and mix until combined.
4. Serve immediately.

Nutrition (per serving)
Calories 102, fat 2.9 g, carbs 15 g, sugar 9.4 g,
Protein 3.2 g, sodium 128 mg

Smoked Butterscotch Latte

This delicious autumn coffee is super easy to make in your home. Enjoy it with a secret ingredient.

Serves 1 | Prep. time 10 minutes

Ingredients
½ cup brewed espresso
1 tablespoon molasses
2 tablespoons butterscotch sauce
¼ cup cream
1 tablespoon brown sugar
¼ cup heavy whipping cream
Pinch of cinnamon

Directions
1. Add the brewed espresso, molasses and butterscotch sauce to a serving glass.
2. Stir in the cream and mix until combined.
3. Whip the whipping cream and brown sugar with a hand mixer and pipe out on top of the glass.
4. Sprinkle cinnamon on top.
5. Serve immediately.

Nutrition (per serving)
Calories 443, fat 14.5 g, carbs 78.7 g, sugar 55.1 g, Protein 1.9 g, sodium 274 mg

Espresso Macchiato

You can easily make this type of coffee in your home with very simple ingredients.

Serves 1 | Prep. time 5 minutes

Ingredients
1 teaspoon ground espresso coffee
1 cup hot water
2–3 tablespoons hot milk
2 tablespoons milk

Directions
1. Brew the espresso in a coffee machine.
2. Add the brewed espresso to a serving glass and stir in the hot milk.
3. Froth the milk in a frother and decorate the glass with the milk foam.
4. Serve and enjoy.

Nutrition (per serving)
Calories 28, fat 0.9 g, carbs 2.3 g, sugar 2.1 g,
Protein 1.8 g, sodium 55 mg

Dark Chocolate Mocha

Rich in flavor, this chocolate coffee is everything you will need to sweeten your busy day.

Serves 1 | Prep. time 5 minutes

Ingredients
1 teaspoon ground espresso coffee
¾ cup water
¾ cup milk
2 tablespoons sugar
½ teaspoon vanilla extract
2 tablespoons cocoa powder
¼ cup whipped cream
1 teaspoon powdered sugar

Directions
1. Brew the espresso in a coffee machine.
2. In a pot, warm the milk, sugar, vanilla, and cocoa powder.
3. Mix the milk with the brewed espresso and transfer it to a serving glass.
4. Whip the whipping cream and powdered sugar with a hand mixer and decorate the glass with the whipped cream. Serve and enjoy.

Nutrition (per serving)
Calories 312, fat 14.4 g, carbs 42.6 g, sugar 35.2 g, Protein 8.8 g, sodium 124 mg

White Choco-Mocha Latte

One of the best flavor combinations—coffee and white chocolate. Easy and fast to prepare.

Serves 1 | Prep. time 5 minutes

Ingredients
¾ cup brewed espresso, warm
¾ cup warm milk
2 tablespoons sugar
½ teaspoon vanilla extract
1 ounce white chocolate
¼ cup whipped cream
1 teaspoon powdered sugar

Directions
1. Add the brewed espresso, warm milk, sugar, vanilla extract, and white chocolate to a serving glass.
2. Stir until the chocolate is melted and then set aside.
3. In a bowl, whip the whipping cream and powdered sugar with a hand mixer and decorate the glass with the whipped cream.
4. Serve and enjoy.

Nutrition (per serving)
Calories 441, fat 22.1 g, carbs 53.4 g, sugar 51.7 g, Protein 8.5 g, sodium 147 mg

Hazelnut Bianco

Yummy and full of hazelnut flavor, this coffee is a true joy.

Serves 1 | Prep. time 5 minutes

Ingredients
1 teaspoon ground espresso coffee
½ cup water
¼ cup milk
1 tablespoon hazelnut syrup
1 tablespoon grated white chocolate

Directions
1. Brew the espresso in a coffee machine.
2. Add the brewed espresso to a serving glass and mix in the milk.
3. Stir in the hazelnut syrup and decorate the glass with grated white chocolate.
4. Serve and enjoy.

Nutrition (per serving)
Calories 120, fat 7.5 g, carbs 10.1 g, sugar 3.5 g, Protein 3.5 g, sodium 55 mg

Cloud Macchiato

Airy and flavorful at the same time, this coffee will wake you up every morning from now on.

Serves 1 | Prep. time 5 minutes

Ingredients
1 teaspoon ground espresso coffee
½ cup warm water
¼ cup milk
1 teaspoon milk powder
½ teaspoon powdered sugar
¼ cup heavy whipping cream
1 teaspoon caramel sauce

Directions
1. Brew the espresso in the coffee machine.
2. Add the milk, milk powder, powdered sugar, and whipping cream to a bowl.
3. Whip with a hand mixer until soft peaks form. Add the mixture on top of the warm coffee in a serving glass.
4. Drizzle with caramel sauce.
5. Serve and enjoy.

Nutrition (per serving)
Calories 168, fat 12.4 g, carbs 11 g, sugar 5.3 g, Protein 3.9 g, sodium 95 mg

Coconut Milk Latte

After you make this tropical flavored coffee, sit down and enjoy every sip of its delicious warmth.

Serves 1 | Prep. time 5 minutes

Ingredients
1 teaspoon ground espresso coffee
¾ cup water
½ cup coconut milk
1 tablespoon brown sugar

Directions
1. Brew the espresso in a coffee machine.
2. Stir in the brown sugar.
3. Steam the coconut milk and then microwave it for about 20 seconds on medium.
4. Add the coconut milk on top of the brewed espresso.
5. Serve and enjoy.

Nutrition (per serving)
Calories 314, fat 28.6 g, carbs 15.5 g, sugar 12.7 g, Protein 3 g, sodium 46 mg

Irish Coffee

This Irish whiskey-infused coffee will wake you up and help you keep going on busy days.

Serves 1 | Prep. time 10 minutes

Ingredients
1 cup brewed coffee, hot
1 tablespoon brown sugar
3 tablespoons Irish whiskey
¼ cup heavy whipping cream
1 teaspoon powdered sugar

Directions
1. Add the brewed coffee and brown sugar to a serving glass.
2. Stir in the whiskey and mix until combined.
3. Whip the whipping cream and powdered sugar until soft peaks form and decorate the glass with it.
4. Serve and enjoy.

Nutrition (per serving)
Calories 256, fat 11.1 g, carbs 12.2 g, sugar 11.3 g, Protein 0.9 g, sodium 46 mg

Americano

This classic American coffee will wake you up whenever you are not in the mood.

Serves 1 | Prep. time 10 minutes

Ingredients
¼ cup brewed espresso, hot
¼ cup boiling water

Directions
1. Add the boiling water to a glass.
2. Brew some strong espresso in an espresso machine and pour it into the glass with the water.
3. Serve and enjoy.

Nutrition (per serving)
Calories 1, fat 0 g, carbs 0 g, sugar 0 g,
Protein 0.1 g, sodium 10 mg

Doppio Coffee

Doppio coffee is similar to a long espresso, but I find it easier to make this way.

Serves 1 | Prep. time 10 minutes

Ingredients
1 tablespoon freshly ground espresso beans
½ cup boiling water

Directions
1. Add the boiling water to a serving glass and stir in the ground espresso.
2. Mix until nice and smooth.
3. Serve and enjoy.

Nutrition (per serving)
Calories 1, fat 0 g, carbs 0 g, sugar 0 g,
Protein 0 g, sodium 4 mg

Nutella Macchiato

This coffee will not only warm you and keep you awake but will also tickle your taste buds.

Serves 1 | Prep. time 10 minutes

Ingredients
½ cup brewed coffee, hot
¼ cup warm milk
2 tablespoons Nutella
½ teaspoon vanilla extract

Directions
1. Add the brewed coffee to a serving glass and stir in the Nutella.
2. Mix until melted and then stir in the warm milk and vanilla.
3. Mix and serve.

Nutrition (per serving)
Calories 438, fat 23.3 g, carbs 49.3 g, sugar 43 g, Protein 6.1 g, sodium 62 mg

Cocoa Powder Infused Espresso

The chocolate hit will make you feel like you are drinking hot cocoa, but you are filling yourself with enough caffeine to stay in a good mood.

Serves 1 | Prep. time 10 minutes

Ingredients
½ cup brewed coffee, hot
1 tablespoon cocoa powder
¼ cup whipped cream
1 teaspoon powdered sugar

Directions
1. Add the brewed coffee to a serving glass and mix it with the cocoa powder.
2. Whip the whipping cream and powdered sugar with a hand mixer and serve on top of the coffee.

Nutrition (per serving)
Calories 111, fat 10 g, carbs 6.3 g, sugar 2.6 g, Protein 1.8 g, sodium 14 mg

Almond Infused Espresso

An almond hit in espresso is a match made in heaven. I love this flavor combination and I hope you are going to love it too.

Serves 1 | Prep. time 10 minutes

Ingredients
1 teaspoon ground espresso coffee
¾ cup hot water
½ teaspoon almond extract
¼ cup almond milk

Directions
1. Brew the espresso in a coffee machine.
2. Add the brewed espresso to a serving glass and stir in the almond extract.
3. Pour in the almond milk and mix until combined.
4. Serve and enjoy.

Nutrition (per serving)
Calories 146, fat 14.3 g, carbs 3.6 g, sugar 2.3 g, Protein 1.6 g, sodium 13 mg

Paprika Infused Coffee

This might be a strange flavor combination, but you don't really taste the paprika in this recipe—it only brings out the coffee flavor more in every sip.

Serves 1 | Prep. time 10 minutes

Ingredients
¾ cup brewed coffee, hot
½ teaspoon paprika powder
1 tablespoon heavy cream

Directions
1. Add the brewed coffee to a serving glass and stir in the paprika powder.
2. Mix in the heavy cream and stir.
3. Serve and enjoy.

Nutrition (per serving)
Calories 57, fat 5.7 g, carbs 1 g, sugar 0.1 g, Protein 0.7 g, sodium 10 mg

Mexican Coffee

Indulge in this yummy coffee with super flavorful combinations. Delicious and super easy to make.

Serves 1 | Prep. time 10 minutes

Ingredients
1 teaspoon ground coffee
¾ cup hot water
2 ounces chocolate, diced
¼ cup milk
1 tablespoon orange peel
1 cinnamon stick
½ teaspoon vanilla extract

Directions
1. Brew the espresso in a coffee machine.
2. Add the brewed coffee to a pitcher and stir in the cinnamon stick, diced chocolate, and orange peel.
3. Let sit until the chocolate is melted.
4. Stir and strain the coffee through a fine-mesh sieve into a serving glass.
5. Fill the glass with milk.
6. Serve and enjoy.

Nutrition (per serving)
Calories 353, fat 18.2 g, carbs 40.3 g, sugar 32.3 g, Protein 6.7 g, sodium 78 mg

Coffee and Cream

This yummy coffee will really wake up all your senses.

Serves 1 | Prep. time 10 minutes

Ingredients
1 teaspoon ground espresso coffee
¾ cup hot water
¼ cup heavy whipping cream
1 teaspoon powdered sugar

Directions
1. Brew the espresso in a coffee machine.
2. Add the brewed espresso to a serving cup.
3. Whip the heavy cream and powdered sugar with a hand mixer until stiff peaks form.
4. Add dollops of the whipped cream to the coffee, stirring carefully.
5. Serve and enjoy.

Nutrition (per serving)
Calories 115, fat 11.1 g, carbs 3.3 g, sugar 2.5 g, Protein 0.8 g, sodium 15 mg

Hot Mocha Float

Delicious and super easy to make, this floating coffee will inspire you to use your imagination to create something so simple but delicious at the same time.

Serves 1 | Prep. time 10 minutes

Ingredients
1 teaspoon ground espresso coffee
¾ cup hot water
2 tablespoons sugar
¼ cup milk
2 scoops chocolate ice cream

Directions
1. Brew the espresso in a coffee machine.
2. Add the brewed espresso to a serving cup.
3. Stir in the sugar and milk and serve the cup with the chocolate ice cream.

Nutrition (per serving)
Calories 396, fat 15.3 g, carbs 59 g, sugar 54.8 g, Protein 6.8 g, sodium 138 mg

Cinnamon Cappuccino

If you are a big fan of cappuccino coffee, this cinnamon version will make you love it even more.

Serves 1 | Prep. time 10 minutes

Ingredients
2 tablespoons vanilla cappuccino powder
½ teaspoon ground cinnamon
¼ cup warm milk
1 cup boiling water

Directions
1. Add the cappuccino powder, ground cinnamon, and warm milk to a serving cup.
2. Stir and pour in the boiling water.
3. Stir again and serve.

Nutrition (per serving)
Calories 513, fat 13.3 g, carbs 87.9 g, sugar 86.8 g, Protein 14.1 g, sodium 206 mg

Vietnamese Egg Coffee

This Asian coffee is super easy to make. You might change your classic espresso coffee and replace it with this one.

Serves 1 | Prep. time 10 minutes

Ingredients
1 cup brewed coffee, hot
2 tablespoons sugar
1 egg yolk

Directions
1. Add the brewed coffee to a serving cup and stir in the egg yolk and sugar.
2. Mix until combined and serve.

Nutrition (per serving)
Calories 146, fat 4.6 g, carbs 24.6 g, sugar 24.1 g, Protein 3 g, sodium 3 mg

Café au Lait

Easy to make with just a mug and spoon, this coffee will become one of your favorites.

Serves 1 | Prep. time 10 minutes

Ingredients
2 teaspoons ground espresso coffee
1 cup hot water
½ cup warm milk
1 tablespoon sugar
1 teaspoon cocoa powder for serving

Directions
1. Brew the espresso in a coffee machine.
2. Add the brewed coffee to a serving cup and stir in the warm milk and sugar.
3. Mix until combined and dust with cocoa powder to serve.

Nutrition (per serving)
Calories 112, fat 2.8 g, carbs 19 g, sugar 17.5 g, Protein 4.6 g, sodium 63 mg

Caramel Affogato

This is a super easy to make and super delicious caramel infused coffee.

Serves 1 | Prep. time 10 minutes

Ingredients
2 teaspoons finely ground espresso
½ cup water
2 scoops caramel ice cream
¼ cup warm milk

Directions
1. Brew the espresso in a coffee machine.
2. Add the brewed coffee and caramel ice cream to a lidded jar.
3. Mix until the ice cream is melted and then pour the mixture into a mug.
4. Add the warm milk, stir and serve.

Nutrition (per serving)
Calories 352, fat 17.3 g, carbs 45 g, sugar 38.8 g, Protein 6.1 g, sodium 211 mg

RECIPE INDEX

COOKING CONVERSION
CHARTS

1. Measuring Equivalent Chart

Type	Imperial	Imperial	Metric
Weight	1 dry ounce		28g
	1 pound	16 dry ounces	0.45 kg
Volume	1 teaspoon		5 ml
	1 dessert spoon	2 teaspoons	10 ml
	1 tablespoon	3 teaspoons	15 ml
	1 Australian tablespoon	4 teaspoons	20 ml
	1 fluid ounce	2 tablespoons	30 ml
	1 cup	16 tablespoons	240 ml
	1 cup	8 fluid ounces	240 ml
	1 pint	2 cups	470 ml
	1 quart	2 pints	0.95 l
	1 gallon	4 quarts	3.8 l
Length	1 inch		2.54 cm

Numbers are rounded to the closest equivalent

2. Oven Temperature Equivalent Chart

Fahrenheit (°F)	Celsius (°C)	Gas Mark
220	100	
225	110	1/4
250	120	1/2
275	140	1
300	150	2
325	160	3
350	180	4
375	190	5
400	200	6
425	220	7
450	230	8
475	250	9
500	260	

* Celsius (°C) = T (°F)-32] * 5/9

** Fahrenheit (°F) = T (°C) * 9/5 + 32

*** Numbers are rounded to the closest equivalent

Made in United States
Troutdale, OR
10/15/2024

23774019R00037